INUIT

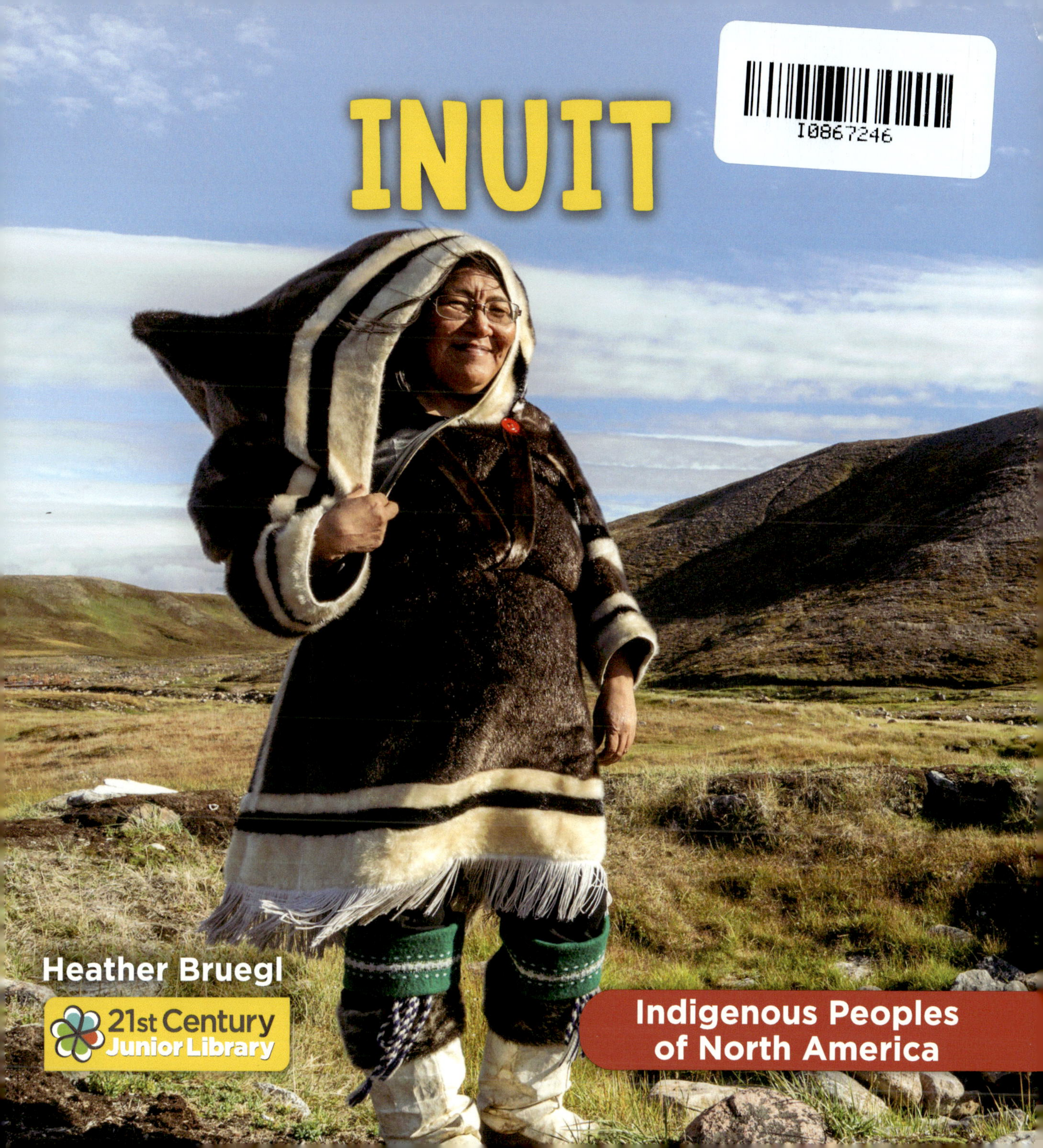

Heather Bruegl

21st Century Junior Library

Indigenous Peoples of North America

Published in the United States of America by:

CHERRY LAKE PRESS
2395 South Huron Parkway, Suite 200, Ann Arbor, Michigan 48104
www.cherrylakepress.com

Reading Adviser: Beth Walker Gambro, MS, Ed., Reading Consultant, Yorkville, IL
Content Advisor: June 'Ashana' Thiele, Dena'ina-Athabascan/Yup'ik

Photo Credits: © robertharding/Alamy, cover, title page; © Sergey Uryadnikov/Shutterstock, 5; © AlexUm5/Shutterstock, 6; © Sabena Jane Blackbird/Alamy, 8–9; © lippyjr/iStock, 10; © Gerry Broome/ASSOCIATED PRESS, 11; © photostaud/Alamy, 13; © Galyna Andrushko, Shutterstock, 14; © Melissa Renwick/REUTERS, 17; © Stephanie Foden, 19; © Danita Delimont/Alamy, 21

Cherry Lake Press is an imprint of Cherry Lake Publishing Group.

Library of Congress Cataloging-in-Publication Data has been filed and is available at catalog.loc.gov

Cherry Lake Publishing Group would like to acknowledge the work of the Partnership for 21st Century Learning, a Network of Battelle for Kids. Please visit Battelle for Kids online for more information.

Printed in the United States of America

Note from publisher: Websites change regularly, and their future contents are outside of our control. Supervise children when conducting any recommended online searches for extended learning opportunities.

About the Content Advisor: June 'Ashana' Thiele is an Emmy-nominated (*Molly of Denali*) writer and actor. They are Yup'ik and Dena'ina Athabascan from Alaska and live in Michigan with their wife and two children.

CHERRY LAKE PRESS

CONTENTS

WHO WE ARE

The word *Inuit* (IH-nyoo-it) means "the people" in Inuktut. Inuktut is the collection of Inuit languages and **dialects**. The Inuit are Indigenous peoples. They have lived in Arctic areas for thousands of years. Inuit belong to different communities. In Canada, Inuit is a legal status. The Canadian Constitution recognizes three sets of Indigenous peoples: First Nations, Inuit, and **Métis**.

In Canada, there are Inuit communities in the Inuvialuit Settlement Region, Nunavut, Nunavik, and Nunatsiavut. Different groups can have their own names, traditions, and languages. In the United States, these groups include the Iñupiat, Yup'ik, and others. In Greenland, they include the Kalaallit.

Inuit stone figures like this, called an *inuksuk*, guide travelers across the Arctic.

Think!

How important do you think knowledge of the land is to people who live in the Arctic? Explain your answer.

Wherever they live, Inuit are related through their **culture**. The Inuit worldview is called *Inuit Qaujimajatuqangit* (IH-nyoo-it kye-YOO-mye-yah-too-kahn-git). It includes the core **values** that guide them.

They value working for the **common good**. They respect all living things and try to live in harmony and balance. They plan and prepare for the future. Part of this is sharing knowledge and being **resourceful**. It also includes working together **in community** to make decisions.

OUR LIVES TODAY

Between 160,000 to 180,000 Inuit live around the world. Most live in Canada. Around 9,000 Inuit live in the United States. Around 55,000 Inuit live in Greenland. Most communities have land claim agreements. These agreements are made with national governments. The agreements help protect Indigenous rights to the land and to **self-govern**.

Inuit traditions and culture are important parts of Inuit life today. Traditional hunting and fishing still **sustain** many Inuit communities. Inuit women may wear *kakiniit* (kah-ki-NEET), or ceremonial tattoos. This tattooing practice was once **banned**. Inuit women are reclaiming it.

Inuit are found in all professions, from doctors to **activists** to actors. Many serve or have served in the Canadian or U.S. military.

Benno Cleveland is an Iñupiaq Army veteran. He founded the Alaska Native Veterans Association.

Callan Chythlook-Sifsof made Olympic history.

Callan Chythlook-Sifsof is an Olympic snowboarder. She is Inuit and Yup'ik. She was the first Alaskan Native to compete in the Olympics.

Kenojuak Ashevak is a famous Inuit artist. She brought Inuit art to people all over the world. Osuitok Ipeelee is a sculptor. His work shows the delicate and graceful nature of Arctic wildlife.

Sheila Watt-Cloutier is an Inuit activist. She works on environmental issues affecting Arctic peoples. She shares how **climate change** puts the Inuit way of life at risk.

Inuit provide for their families and communities every day. They work to preserve their language. They share their skills and knowledge. They protect the environment.

Ask Questions!

What other questions do you have about Inuit life today? Make a plan to find answers.

This Inuit father teaches his son about tracking seals under the ice.

The Arctic is home to many different plants and animals that the Inuit depend on.

OUR ANCESTRAL LANDS

Inuit ancestral land is called *Inuit Nunangat* (NOO-nuhn-ghaht). This large territory spans different countries. It stretches from Russia through the U.S. state of Alaska, the Arctic regions of Canada, and parts of Greenland. Arctic life is different. There are months without sun in some places. Those same places have months when the sun does not set. Inuit communities thrive because they understand the land. It is part of who they are.

The Inuit hunt land animals such as caribou and musk ox. In the sea, they fish and hunt animals such as seals, whales, and walruses. They also gather berries and different plants during the summer months.

Caring for the land is extremely important to the Inuit, but they face environmental challenges today. Climate change is rapidly affecting the Arctic. Ice is melting and sea levels are rising. Traveling is more dangerous.

Look!

Find pictures of the Arctic from long ago and from today. How has the land changed?

Rex Holwell is Inuit. He uses technology to track ice thickness so Inuit travelers can stay safe.

Hunting and gathering food is harder because animal **migration** patterns are changing. Climate change also causes coastal **erosion**. This puts homes and buildings at risk. The Inuit people work hard for policies that will help them protect the lands that they call home.

CARRYING TRADITIONS FORWARD

The Inuit have a rich and vibrant culture. Communities dance, drum, and sing together. They tell stories. Traditional art forms are still practiced today. Inuit throat singing began as a game women played. They did this while men were on hunting trips. Today, Inuit throat singers blend traditional styles with modern music. They share the tradition with people around the world.

Shina Novalinga (right) is a traditional Inuit throat singer and social media influencer. Novalinga began throat singing with her mother (left) when she was 7.

Inuit sculpture is another art form with a long history. Walrus ivory, whale bones, and soapstone are carved into distinctive shapes and figures.

The Inuit craft clothes that are warm and strong enough for Arctic winters. Skilled needleworkers decorate parkas, mittens, and other clothing with bright, detailed designs.

Create!

Design your own Arctic clothing. Draw a picture of your idea. Add designs that represent you and your family or community.

This Inuit grandfather builds a traditional winter igloo as his 4-year-old granddaughter watches.

Traditional celebrations and ceremonies give thanks and express hope for the future. *Quviasukviks* (koo-vee-AH-sook-vik) is a winter festival and feast. It means "happy day." It celebrates daylight lasting longer. Families and communities gather. They celebrate the past year and welcome the new year.

Each tradition the Inuit pass on keeps their culture and people strong.

GLOSSARY

activists (AK-tih-vists) people who openly take action to support a cause

banned (BAND) made illegal by those in power

climate change (KLIE-muht CHAYNJ) significant disruption in Earth's climate and weather patterns that impact land, water, and animal seasonal patterns

common good (KAH-muhn GUHD) that which benefits all

culture (KUHL-chuhr) the language, customs, ideas, and art of a particular group of people

dialects (DIE-uh-lekts) regional varieties of a language with different words, grammar, and pronunciation

erosion (ih-ROH-zhuhn) wearing of Earth's surface by wind or water

in community (IHN kuh-MYOO-nuh-tee) Indigenous concept of being open to and connected with one's community on a deep level

Métis (may-TEEZ) an Indigenous people in Canada with a distinct culture and history stemming from the union of First Nations and European peoples

migration (mie-GRAY-shuhn) the regular, seasonal movement of animals from one habitat to another

resourceful (rih-SORS-fuhl) able to use knowledge, such as Indigenous knowledge, to solve problems and persist despite hardship

self-govern (self-GUH-vern) to lead and manage one's own self or group

sustain (suh-STAYN) strengthen and support

values (VAL-yooz) important principles, morals, or beliefs

FIND OUT MORE

Books

Tidwell, Tia. *The Inuit: People, Culture, and History.* North Mankato, MN: Capstone, 2026.

Sorell, Traci. *We Are Still Here! Native American Truths Everyone Should Know.* Watertown, MA: Charlesbridge, 2021.

Online

With an adult, explore more online with these suggested searches.

- "ICC Kids, Fun Facts," Inuit Circumpolar Council
- "Inuktut Tusâlanga," Piruvik, Government of Nanuvut

Say Hello!

Tunngasugit (TOON-guh-soo-geet), *Tunngahugit* (toon-guh-HOO-geet), or *Tunngahuglutit* (toon-guh-HOO-teet) are Inuit greetings that mean "Welcome." They are spelled differently because there are many dialects of Inuktuk.

INDEX

ABOUT THE AUTHOR

Heather Bruegl, a member of the Oneida Nation of Wisconsin/Stockbridge-Munsee, is a Madonna University graduate with a Master of Arts in U.S. History. She is a public historian and decolonial educator, and her Munsee name is Kiishookunkwe, meaning "Sunflower in Full Bloom." Heather frequently travels to present on Indigenous history, policy, and activism, bringing her deep knowledge and personal connection to the subject.